USBORNE
POMPEII
Picture Book

Struan Reid

Illustrated by Aleks Sennwald & Ian McNee

Designed by Tom Lalonde & Emily Barden

Consultant: Dr. Anne Millard

CONTENTS

DEATH OF A CITY

On the morning of August 24, in the year 79, Mount Vesuvius, a volcano in southern Italy that had been silent for decades, suddenly burst into life and exploded. By the end of the following day, the cities of Pompeii and Herculaneum were buried under ash, rock and mud, where they remained – lost and largely forgotten – for the next 1,700 years.

POMPEII AND THE ROMAN EMPIRE

At the time of the eruption, Pompeii was a rich and bustling city of 20,000 people, an important trading port at the heart of the Roman empire. The Romans, who controlled Italy and much of the Mediterranean, were near the height of their power, and riches poured in from faraway lands. This map shows some of the main Roman cities.

Although Vesuvius destroyed Pompeii and the surrounding area, it preserved in ash a vivid picture of life in a Roman city. Most of the city would have decayed long ago, or been built over, if the volcano hadn't erupted and buried it.

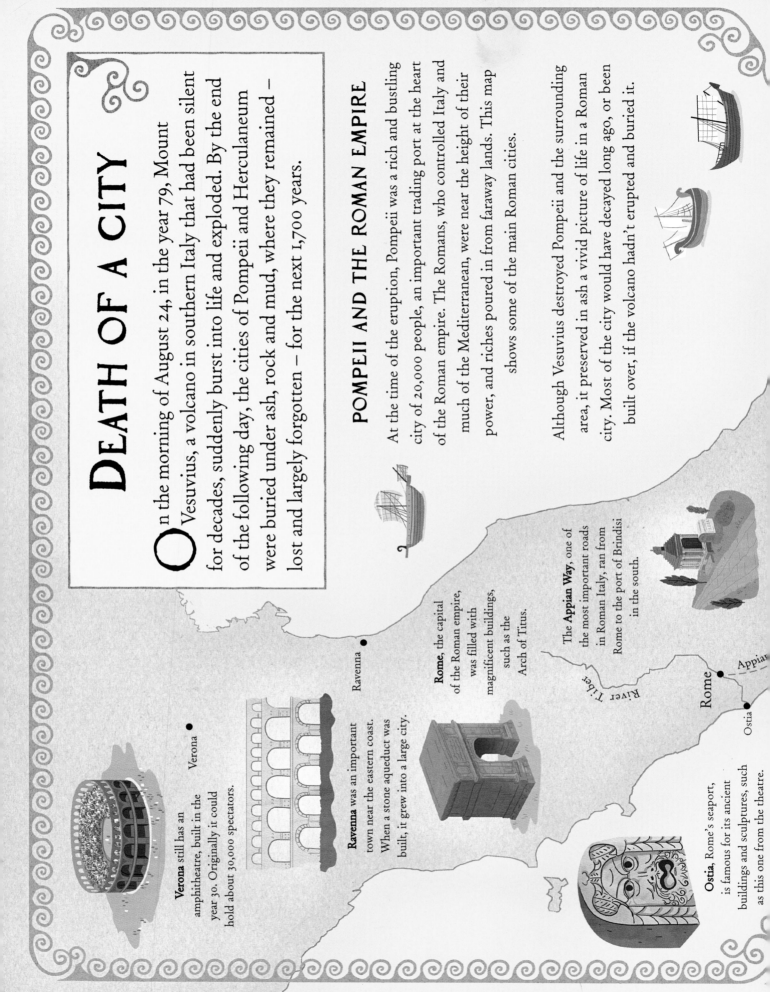

Verona still has an amphitheatre, built in the year 30. Originally it could hold about 30,000 spectators.

Ravenna was an important town near the eastern coast. When a stone aqueduct was built, it grew into a large city.

Rome, the capital of the Roman empire, was filled with magnificent buildings, such as the Arch of Titus.

The Appian Way, one of the most important roads in Roman Italy, ran from Rome to the port of Brindisi in the south.

Ostia, Rome's seaport, is famous for its ancient buildings and sculptures, such as this one from the theatre.

Verona

Ravenna

River Tiber

Rome

Appian

Ostia

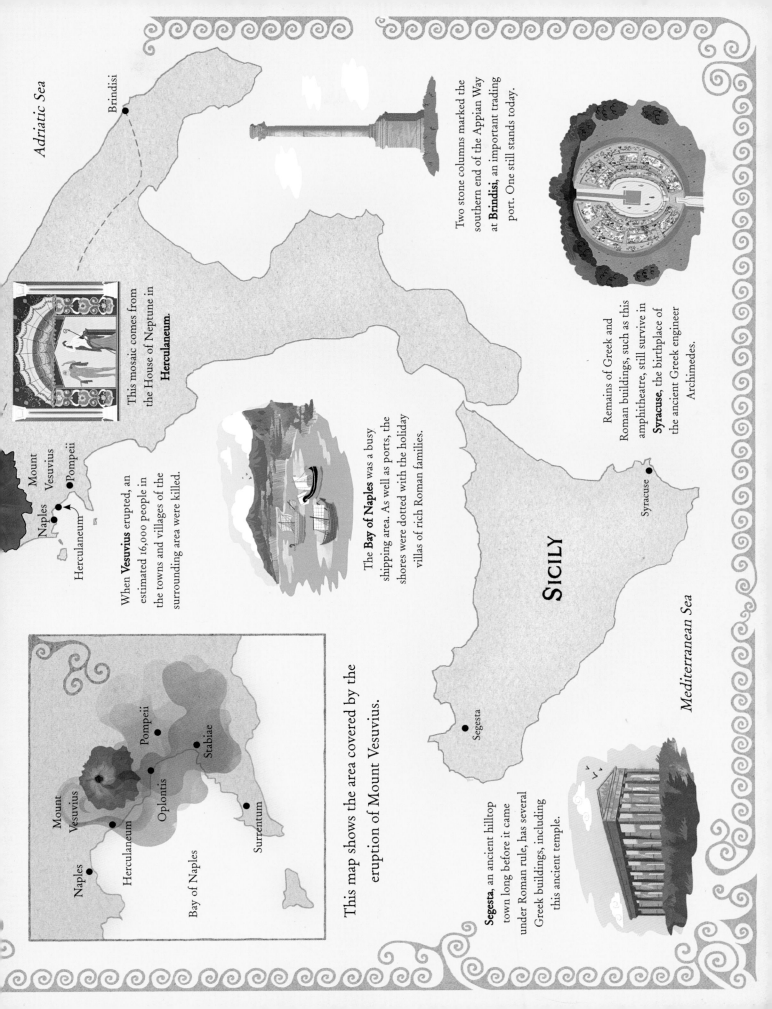

Adriatic Sea

Brindisi

This mosaic comes from the House of Neptune in **Herculaneum.**

Two stone columns marked the southern end of the Appian Way at **Brindisi,** an important trading port. One still stands today.

Mount Vesuvius

Pompeii

Naples

Herculaneum

When **Vesuvius** erupted, an estimated 16,000 people in the towns and villages of the surrounding area were killed.

The **Bay of Naples** was a busy shipping area. As well as ports, the shores were dotted with the holiday villas of rich Roman families.

Remains of Greek and Roman buildings, such as this amphitheatre, still survive in **Syracuse,** the birthplace of the ancient Greek engineer Archimedes.

Syracuse

SICILY

Mediterranean Sea

Segesta

Segesta, an ancient hilltop town long before it came under Roman rule, has several Greek buildings, including this ancient temple.

This map shows the area covered by the eruption of Mount Vesuvius.

Naples

Mount Vesuvius

Herculaneum

Pompeii

Oplontis

Stabiae

Surrentum

Bay of Naples

POMPEII AD79

At the time of its destruction, Pompeii was a flourishing city full of contrasts. Splendid public buildings and luxurious houses with gardens sat crammed alongside narrow, dirty streets lined with shops and overcrowded apartment blocks.

A silver hand mirror found at the House of Menander

If you wanted to enter the city, you had a choice of eight gateways to go through. The **Marine Gate** led towards the port, so most of the city's trade passed this way.

High stone walls surrounded the city – built in pre-Roman times to protect it from attack.

The **House of the Vettii** and **House of the Faun** were two of the most luxurious houses to have survived, full of wall paintings.

The **Central Baths** were the latest of five bath complexes in Pompeii, built after an earthquake in 62.

Important sites

1. Marine Gate
2. Basilica
3. Forum
4. Temple of Jupiter
5. Forum Baths
6. House of the Faun
7. House of the Vettii
8. Central Baths
9. Large Theatre
10. Small Theatre
11. Gladiators' barracks
12. House of Menander
13. Street of Abundance
14. Palaestra
15. Amphitheatre

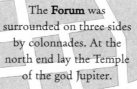

The **Forum** was surrounded on three sides by colonnades. At the north end lay the Temple of the god Jupiter.

The **House of Menander** was a grand villa. It got its name from a wall painting found inside showing an ancient Greek writer named Menander.

4

THE FORUM

The main temples and official buildings were all built near the Forum. This was also where most of Pompeii's business dealings went on – in the merchants' warehouses and offices tucked away behind the colonnades.

This fresco shows a baker named Terentius Neo and his wife, holding a scroll and wax tablet for writing on.

The Forum was dotted with statues of important citizens and historical figures – sometimes on horseback. This fresco shows people walking past some of them.

A TRADING CITY

Pompeii's main products were wine, wool and olive oil, and its wealthiest citizens were merchants and bankers.

The **Street of Abundance** was one of the oldest and most important streets in Pompeii. It connected the Forum to the eastern part of the city. ⑬

The **Palaestra** was an exercise area next to the **Amphitheatre**. It was surrounded on three sides by colonnades.

⑭

⑮

One of the most powerful jobs you could have was to be a senior magistrate, or *duovir*. Two were elected to serve in the city council each year.

This marble statue shows a magistrate named Marcus Holconius Rufus. He was elected *duovir* five times.

This silver wine cup was found in the ruins of the House of Menander.

On market days, traders set up stalls and carts around the Forum from where they sold their goods.

Temple of Jupiter

Covered colonnades provided shelter from the sun and rain, with shops and offices inside.

PUBLIC BUILDINGS

Pompeii was a busy and crowded place, with buildings packed into narrow streets laid out in a grid pattern, and very few open spaces.

THE FORUM

The heart of the city was the Forum, the only large, open area. As well as being the marketplace, it was the headquarters of religion, politics and business too.

This bronze statue of Apollo was found inside the ruins of the Temple of Apollo, just to the west of the Forum.

This mosaic showing street musicians comes from a floor found in a house in Pompeii.

The temple to the god Jupiter, at the north of the Forum, was the most important temple in the city. There were other smaller temples too, such as the Temple of Apollo.

LAW AND ORDER

In the south-west corner was the Basilica, the oldest and most important public building in the city. It was used as the main law court, and business and financial dealings took place there too.

Inside the Basilica was an enormous hall, lined with stone columns.

Criminals were sentenced in the tribunal, which lay at the far end of the main hall.

PUBLIC ENTERTAINMENT

Pompeii had vast buildings designed for public entertainment on a massive scale. The largest, the amphitheatre, could squeeze in up to 20,000 spectators.

This mosaic shows actors getting ready before a play.

The amphitheatre was the site of hugely popular, bloodthirsty fights between gladiators – prisoners trained to fight each other or wild animals. There was also a small theatre, an Odeon, for about a thousand people, and a bigger one for 5,000.

This bronze gladiator's helmet, found in the city ruins, has detailed decoration on top.

The gladiator's head and neck were protected, with covers over his eyes.

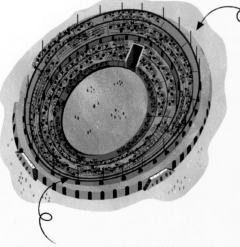

The seats inside the amphitheatre were banked steeply to get more people in.

RELAXING AT THE BATHS

Most houses didn't have bathrooms, so people went to any one of the five public bath houses to wash. They were also seen as great places to relax and gossip with friends.

Canvas awnings could be pulled over the top seats to protect against the sun.

The Romans didn't have soap. Instead, they covered their bodies in oils which they scraped off with curved wood or metal scrapers called *strigils*.

A VILLA IN POMPEII

Most people in Pompeii lived in crowded apartment blocks, known as *insulae*. But wealthier families could afford their own elegant, spacious town house, called a *domus*.

INSIDE A DOMUS

Houses in Pompeii tended to follow the same basic layout, whatever the size. This very grand villa was unusual in having a second floor.

③ Family rooms around a central courtyard, or *impluvium*

④ The kitchen

⑤ Second floor bedrooms

Roof covered in thick clay tiles

The main entrance into the house opened directly onto the street.

① The dining room, or *triclinium*

② Family shrine, or *lararium*

The rooms at the front were often rented out to shopkeepers.

Lavatory

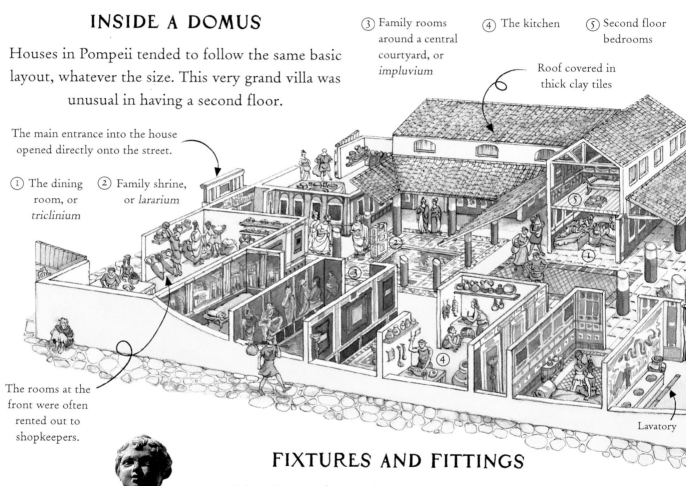

FIXTURES AND FITTINGS

Most Roman houses had much less furniture than houses today. But grand villas, like this one, would have had lots of chairs, tables and couches.

Statues made of stone or bronze, like this one, were dotted around the house and garden.

The most expensive beds, like this wood and bronze one, had feather mattresses.

Rooms were lit by small oil lamps. This one is made of solid gold, but most were pottery or bronze. Some houses had tall bronze standard lamps or hanging lanterns.

WALLS AND FLOORS

Surviving houses from Pompeii tell us a lot about how Roman houses would have been decorated. Many of the walls were covered – floor to ceiling – with wall paintings. Floors were often decorated with mosaics – patterns or scenes made from thousands of small cut stones.

This wall painting was designed to make the room it was in feel bigger than it really was.

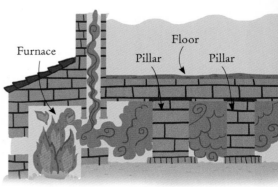

Some houses in Pompeii even had central heating. Hot air passed from a furnace through channels under the floor and inside the walls.

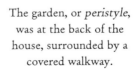

Bathroom

The garden, or *peristyle*, was at the back of the house, surrounded by a covered walkway.

This mosaic of a dog was found on the floor of one of the Pompeii houses.

Mosaic floors were made up of scenes or decorated with elaborate patterns.

GARDENS

Gardens were filled with flowers and small trees, such as figs and pomegranates, and there were fountains to keep the air cool in the summer heat.

This detail from a wall painting from a house in Pompeii shows birds in a tree near a garden fountain.

Rich Pompeiians would stroll around under shady colonnades.

TRADES AND CRAFTS

The streets of Pompeii were packed with small workshops of every sort. Craftsmen worked at the back of them, and sold their goods at the front.

WOOLLEN GOODS

One of the most important industries in Pompeii was the manufacture of wool, which came from sheep grazing in the hills behind the city. Fullers prepared the wool, and then passed it to spinners, who turned it into yarn for clothes and blankets.

This wall painting, from one of the houses in Pompeii, shows fullers washing wool.

Weavers – often women working at home – wove the yarn into lengths of cloth.

This mosaic of a storage jar, advertising fish sauce, was found in a Pompeii shop.

POTTERIES

Wine was an important export. Large pottery jars, called amphoras, were made to transport wine all around the Mediterranean.

To make his pots, the potter turned the top wheel by kicking the stone wheel at his feet.

This elaborate glass amphora shows people drinking wine among grapevines.

GETTING TO WORK

From early in the morning until late at night, the streets were busy with people going to and from work. Most people walked, but some travelled by ferry from other places along the coast.

This mosaic shows a ferryman taking people to work.

A very rich Pompeiian could afford to hire slaves to carry her through the streets in a litter.

METALWORKERS

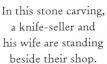

In this stone carving, a knife-seller and his wife are standing beside their shop.

Some workshops echoed with the sound of crashing and bashing, as metalworkers hammered tools, knives, pots and pans from copper, iron and bronze. Others specialized in delicate work in gold and silver.

This is a blacksmith hammering a hot bronze blade into a knife.

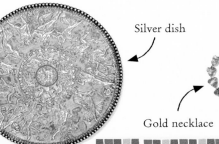

Silver dish

Gold necklace

CARPENTERS

Although most people owned only a few pieces of furniture, carpenters were in demand to make elaborate chairs, tables and storage chests for richer households. Carpenters worked in the building trade and in shipbuilding too.

This carpenter, working with a hammer and chisel, comes from a wall painting.

Buildings were put up using wooden scaffolding, cranes and winches.

FARMING AND FOOD

The land around Pompeii was ideal for farming as the soil was rich in minerals from the nearby volcano.

This wall painting shows a glass bowl piled high with typical local fruit – apples, pomegranates and grapes.

FRESH FROM THE FIELD

Many farms grew a variety of crops. Wheat, oats and barley were grown to make bread and porridge, which was the staple diet of most Pompeiians. Fruit and vegetables included apples, figs and pears, as well as cabbages, lettuce, carrots and radishes.

WINE AND OIL

Most local farms had vines and olive trees. Grapes for wine were cultivated in vineyards, while sweet grapes for eating were often grown inside the farm courtyard.

Carved marble panel showing grapes being pressed for wine

Floor mosaic showing a bunch of grapes

A cargo of wine and olive oil from Pompeii is loaded onto a trade ship.

BIRDS AND BEASTS

Farmers kept chickens, and sometimes ducks and geese, for their eggs and meat. Pigeons were a good source of meat too. Sheep and goats were raised for their milk, which was drunk fresh or turned into cheese. Sheep's wool was sent to the fullers in Pompeii, while goat hair was used to make ropes and sacks.

On this carved stone panel, you can see a fruit market at the top, and farmers tilling the soil below.

Wall painting of a couple of partridge and a dish of eggs

DOWN ON THE FARM

Farmhouses and farm buildings were often surrounded by a walled courtyard. This was where the grape and olive pressing was done. There was usually a dovecote, grain stores and beehives for honey too.

① A beekeeper collects honey.

② Collecting grapes for the table

③ Filling wine vats

④ Pigeons and their dovecote

⑤ Farm workers press olives for oil.

Barn for storage

WINING AND DINING

People in Pompeii started the day with a light breakfast of bread or wheat biscuits with honey. Lunch was eggs, cheese or fruit, and the main meal, the *cena*, came in the late afternoon, after a hard day's work.

SIMPLE FARE

Most people could only afford very simple food, such as porridge and vegetable stews. Sometimes, on special occasions, they cooked roast meat.

A busy day at a food market in Pompeii

Fishing boats brought in their catch every morning. This mosaic shows the wide variety of fish that was available.

STREET FOOD

Most people lived in crowded apartment blocks, with no room for a kitchen. They bought meals from restaurants or street stalls.

Hot sausages, stews, sweet pastries and bread were sold from street restaurants.

The hot food counters in the restaurant of Vetutis Placidus in Pompeii

A DINNER PARTY

In wealthy families, guests were often invited to the afternoon *cena*. Sumptuous dishes and musicians and singers were arranged to entertain them.

The guests reclined on couches in the *triclinium*, while servants brought in the food and wine. This wall painting shows a servant bringing in a plate of food.

Diners recline on couches.

Servant bringing more wine

Porters collect jars of wine from the store rooms before serving.

SWEET WINES

Wine was stored in large pottery amphoras before being brought to the table in smaller jugs. It was usually mixed with water and sweetened with honey and spices.

Guests sipped from this silver cup, decorated with olive branches, which was passed around them.

DAILY BREAD

Bakers in Pompeii set up stalls in the market or sold bread direct from the bakery itself. There were more than 30 bakeries in the city and customers gathered early every morning.

This loaf of bread was found in the ruins of Pompeii.

This wall painting shows people collecting bread from a bakery.

Bakers grind the grain before making the loaves.

GODS OF POMPEII

The people of Pompeii, like all Romans, worshipped many different gods and goddesses. Archaeologists have uncovered sculptures and paintings of some of their gods among the ruins of the city.

THE BIG NAMES

Each god or goddess controlled a different aspect of life or nature. The three most important ones were Jupiter, Juno and Minerva.

Jupiter was king of the gods, ruler of the skies and god of thunder and lightning.

Jupiter is often shown holding a thunderbolt in his raised hand, ready to strike down his enemies.

Juno was the wife and sister of Jupiter, and goddess of women and childbirth.

This wall painting of Juno surrounded by other gods was found on the wall of one of the houses in Pompeii.

Minerva was goddess of crafts and war, and looked after soldiers and school children.

This statue shows Minerva wearing a helmet and holding a spear, ready for battle.

Juno was a very jealous goddess. She sent serpents down to Earth to kill the infant Hercules, the son of Jupiter and a human named Alcmene.

SACRIFICIAL OFFERINGS

The Pompeiians offered gifts such as cakes, flowers and statues to their gods, but the most popular offerings were animals. Priests sacrificed oxen, sheep and doves in front of the temples.

Priests examined the animals' internal organs, believing that these revealed the wishes of the god.

This marble panel from the altar of the Temple of Vespasian in Pompeii shows a bull being led to sacrifice. The priest on the left is wearing a veil.

When the god's will was known, the animal's organs were burned in a fire on an altar.

Priests led animals to be sacrificed to the god on an altar in front of the temple.

This detail from a wall painting found in Pompeii shows a bull being led to a temple altar.

WATCHING OVER THE FAMILY

The Pompeiians prayed to household spirits too. *Lares* were spirits who protected the whole family. *Penates* looked after the larder and food cupboards.

Every house had a shrine – called a *lararium* – where the family held daily prayers and offered food and wine to the gods.

Family members lay their offerings on the *lararium* and say prayers to the god.

This is part of a *lararium* found in a house in Pompeii. The family would have placed their gifts on the shelf beneath the painting.

LOOKING GOOD

Wall paintings, sculptures and jewels found in Pompeii have helped give archaeologists an impression of what people looked like and how they dressed in Roman times.

GETTING READY

Like all Romans, Pompeiians took a lot of trouble over their appearance. Some rich women took hours getting ready, helped by slaves who washed and dressed them. Pale skins were fashionable, so they whitened their faces and arms with powdered chalk.

The Romans didn't use soap, but washed their hair in water mixed with herbs, and dressed it in perfumed oils.

Women darkened their eyelids with something called antimony, and painted their lips and cheeks with red plant dye.

These glass jars were used to store ointments and powders.

Most men shaved and cut their hair short. A trip to the barber was an important social occasion, but being shaved could be very painful. The barber's blades weren't always very sharp.

This marble sculpture shows a Pompeiian woman with an elaborate hairstyle. Heated tongs were used to curl hair.

Although not as good as glass, a polished silver hand mirror gave a reasonable reflection.

CLOTHES

In Roman times, fashions changed very little for hundreds of years. The most distinctive item of clothing was a *toga*, worn only by wealthy men.

Out in the countryside, people wore wool tunics over long trousers.

This wall painting from Pompeii shows a man wearing a *toga*, a large semicircular piece of wool cloth folded around his body.

First you draped the *toga* over your left shoulder, then pulled the other end around your back and over the same shoulder.

Women wore plain tunics made of fine linen or wool. Over this they draped a long robe, or *stola*.

This wall painting from Pompeii shows a woman wearing a large square shawl, or *palla*, over her *stola*.

This magnificent necklace, made of gold and set with emeralds and large rough pearls called 'blister' pearls, was found in Pompeii.

FINISHING TOUCHES

The Romans liked wearing jewels. The more territories they conquered, the more materials became available. The best pieces were made of gold, pearls and precious stones, such as emeralds and sapphires.

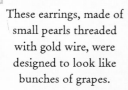

These earrings, made of small pearls threaded with gold wire, were designed to look like bunches of grapes.

The snake was a symbol of healing and protection. Snake designs, like this gold armband, were popular.

GROWING UP

Roman children were brought up to obey their parents and to serve the state. Boys from rich families were trained for a job in the army or government, while girls were expected to marry well and to produce the next generation of loyal citizens.

Rag doll and marbles

A CHILD IS BORN

As many mothers and babies died in childbirth, women married early as it was thought to be safer. It also meant they could have more children – to work and earn money for the family.

Wooden toy horse

Nine days after birth, a child was given a name and a charm, called a *bulla*, to ward off any evil spirits.

TIME FOR GAMES

Roman children played games such as hide-and-seek and leapfrog that many children play today. Their toys included rag dolls and rattles.

GOING TO SCHOOL

Most children received a very basic education before they were sent off to work. Only children from richer families went to school. From six until about 11, boys and girls went to a *ludus*, or elementary school, where they learned reading, writing and arithmetic.

Students sat on low stools in front of the teacher.

IN THE CLASSROOM

School often meant a single room at the back of a house or shop. The school day lasted from dawn until midday without a break. Discipline was strict and pupils could be beaten if they made mistakes or misbehaved. After 11, boys could continue their studies at a secondary school, or *grammaticus*. But girls usually stayed at home and prepared to get married.

This wall painting from Pompeii shows a young girl holding a wooden tablet and *stylus*.

This stone relief shows a teacher surrounded by his students. A class was usually made up of about 12 students.

BOY TO MAN

When a boy reached 14, he was recognized as an adult in a special ceremony. He took off his *bulla*, and was presented with a *toga*. Togas were only worn by adults, so it was a sign that he had grown up.

Many teachers in Roman schools were Greek. Here a teacher is reading through his students' work.

TAKING NOTES

Students scratched out their lessons on wooden tablets covered in wax, using a stick called a *stylus*.

Wooden tablet covered in wax

Stylus

Some important documents were written in ink on a type of paper called *papyrus*.

Students take notes during a lesson.

HEALTH AND MEDICINE

In Roman times, when people were sick they thought they were being punished by the gods. So medical treatment usually combined scientific methods with prayers and offerings to the gods.

MEDICAL TRAINING

Some Pompeiian doctors would have trained in medical schools in Rome. Others learned their skills in army hospitals, where they learned to heal wounds and fix broken bones.

These bronze medical instruments were found in the ruins of Pompeii.

As there were no painkillers, patients drank wine or poppy juice to dull the pain during surgery.

EARLY HISTORY

Pompeiian doctors based their medical knowledge on the writings of ancient Greek doctors. One of the most famous of these was Hippocrates, who lived in the 5th century BC.

Hippocrates gives advice to one of his patients.

This lid from a doctor's instrument box was found in the ruins of Herculaneum. It shows the god Aesculapius and his daughter Hygieia.

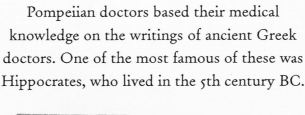

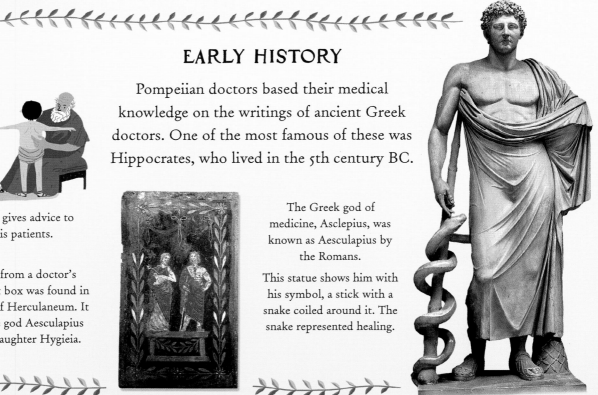

The Greek god of medicine, Asclepius, was known as Aesculapius by the Romans.

This statue shows him with his symbol, a stick with a snake coiled around it. The snake represented healing.

FAMILY DOCTORS

Rich Pompeiians paid a doctor to visit them. But treatment could be very expensive, so most people saw a doctor very rarely.

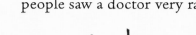

This wall painting shows a famous Greek warrior named Aeneas being treated by a doctor.

There were some travelling doctors who moved from town to town. This doctor has set up his stall in a town square.

SPECIALISTS

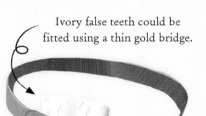

Ivory false teeth could be fitted using a thin gold bridge.

Some doctors were specialists. For example, there were eye doctors who applied ointments made from powdered lead, zinc or iron, mixed with oils. Others looked after teeth.

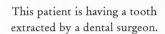

This patient is having a tooth extracted by a dental surgeon.

LOTIONS AND POTIONS

This stone carving shows a pharmacist sitting in her workshop. Behind her, one of her assistants is grinding up ingredients.

Roman medicines were made from wild herbs, plants and minerals and, occasionally, parts of animals. Professional pharmacists sold medicines and ointments, but people often made their own home-made remedies.

This wall painting, from the House of the Vettii in Pompeii, shows small, winged boys, known as *putti*, working in a pharmacist's shop.

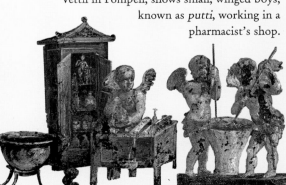

Rosemary was used to soothe eyes.

Fennel calmed nerves.

Sage was used in cough mixtures.

Lemon balm was used for headaches.

ENTERTAINMENT

The Romans had lots of religious holidays. Many poor people had no jobs at all, so public shows were put on at the theatre and amphitheatre, to entertain them – and to keep them out of trouble.

THE GAMES

What the Romans enjoyed most was the popular entertainment known as 'the games'. These were bloodthirsty fights between gladiators or wild animals held in the amphitheatre. Local politicians could make themselves popular by paying for the games and allowing people in for free.

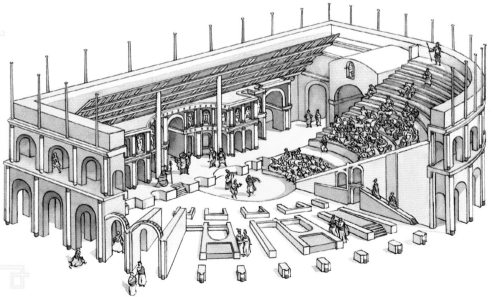

THE THEATRE

There were two theatres in Pompeii. The smaller, older theatre, known as the Odeon, put on serious performances of tragedies (plays with sad endings), lectures and poetry readings. The larger theatre showed popular plays, comedies and concerts.

This statue is of Melpomene, goddess of Tragedy. She is holding a 'tragic' mask in her hand.

Charioteers raced in teams, wearing red, white, blue or green.

A DAY AT THE RACES

Chariot races were exciting and hugely popular too. In the largest Roman cities, they were held in a specially designed stadium called a *circus*. But in Pompeii they usually took place in the amphitheatre or outside the city walls.

This detail of a Pompeii wall painting shows a *quadrigas* (four-horse) chariot race.

HUNTING

The countryside around Pompeii provided many opportunities for hunting wild animals. Rich citizens did this for sport, but for poorer people it could be a useful source of meat for the family.

This is a copy of a wall painting found in Pompeii. It shows hunters stalking various wild animals, including a lion.

Rabbits, deer and boar were hunted with spears and dogs. Slings and stones were used to bring down wild birds.

Some people hunted on their own, but others went out as part of a large hunting party.

GAMES AND MUSIC

At home, families and friends enjoyed playing board games using counters and dice. Small private concerts with music and singing were popular too.

A stone carving showing *putti* playing a board game using dice

This wall painting from Stabiae shows a woman with a musical instrument called a *cithara*.

DESTRUCTION

On a calm, clear morning in the year 79, the volcano Vesuvius started to stir, after years of sleeping. There had been rumblings before, but no-one was prepared for what happened. After the first small eruption, Vesuvius let out a terrifying roar.

RAINING DEATH

A column of fire and red-hot rocks shot into the air and started raining down on the area around Pompeii. A cloud of poisonous gases rolled down the mountain, killing everything in its path. People ran for shelter, but there was nowhere to hide.

In just 18 hours, Vesuvius blasted out billions of tons of rock, killing 5,000 people in Pompeii alone.

NO ESCAPE

Some people fled the city, but they were still battered to death by rocks or poisoned by fumes. Boats in the port quickly filled with people trying to escape across the Bay of Naples, but only a few made it.

GRAB AND RUN

Terrified citizens rushed out into the crowded streets. They grabbed small objects such as jewels and coins and stuffed them into purses.

A few of the objects found scattered in the ruins of Pompeii

This skeleton was found with gold rings set with gemstones.

This mosaic floor was found in a house in Pompeii.

A BLANKET OF ASH

On the second day, as the bombardment of rocks subsided, a thick, choking cloud of volcanic ash settled like a blanket over the wreckage of the city.

Thick clouds of ash spewed out of Vesuvius and smothered everything.

ENTOMBED

Over the following weeks, wind and rain blew across the area and the ash set rock hard. The devastation was so complete that the city was never rebuilt. Pompeii remained hidden inside the ash, like a time capsule.

These are plaster casts of a man and dog killed in the destruction.

AN EYEWITNESS ACCOUNT

A first-hand account by lawyer and writer Pliny the Younger tells us something about what happened. His uncle, Pliny the Elder, military commander of the region, sailed across the bay to try to help, but died when he was overwhelmed by the heat and fumes.

Pliny's uncle's house was at Misenum, 30km (19 miles) across the bay. He watched in horror as he saw the disaster unfold.

HERCULANEUM

On the other side of the volcano from Pompeii was the smaller city of Herculaneum. It too was buried under the ash and lay hidden for the next 1,700 years.

The citizens of Herculaneum ran from the volcano's billowing ash clouds.

DEAD BUT PRESERVED

During the eruption of Vesuvius, the winds blew most of the volcanic rocks and mud towards Pompeii. The buildings in Herculaneum weren't as badly affected, and a number of them have been found intact.

VILLA OF THE PAPYRI

One of the most impressive buildings at Herculaneum is the Villa dei Pisoni, or Villa of the Papyri. It may have belonged to Julius Caesar's father-in-law, Lucius Calpurnius Piso.

A library of 1,800 papyrus scrolls was found inside one of the villa's rooms, badly scorched by the heat.

The design of the Getty Museum in California, USA, is based on a recreation of the Villa dei Pisoni.

This detail of a wall painting from Herculaneum shows a man unrolling a papyrus scroll.

A collection of sculptures was found in the villa, including this bronze statue of Mercury ...

... and this marble bust of Demetrios Poliorketes, King of Macedonia.

CULT OF THE EMPERORS

Another building uncovered at Herculaneum was the College of the Augustales. It was home to a college of priests who worshipped the family of the Roman emperors. It contained one large room with wooden roof beams scorched by the heat from the volcano.

The walls of the chamber were painted with scenes of the story of Hercules, the legendary founder of Herculaneum.

This wall painting from Herculaneum shows a mythical creature called a centaur with a Greek hero named Achilles.

PAINTED WALLS

Because many of the buildings at Herculaneum were so well preserved, some of the very best Roman wall paintings have been found inside them. They show scenes of daily life, stories of heroes and gods, and dishes of food.

TRYING TO ESCAPE

For years after the discovery of Herculaneum, people believed that most of the inhabitants must have escaped, as few human remains had been found. But, in 1982, archaeologists discovered hundreds of skeletons huddled together in the port area of town.

People must have run down to the port, hoping to board boats to take them to safety across the Bay of Naples. But as they waited, they were killed by a blast of searing heat from Vesuvius.

DISCOVERY

Farmers occasionally dug up fragments from the two ruined cities, but thought little of it. Then, in 1709, large stones from Herculaneum were accidently uncovered and people rushed to the area to find more.

TREASURE HUNTERS

One of the first people to visit the Herculaneum ruins was Austrian nobleman and art collector, Prince of Elboeuf. But he was really only interested in looking for sculptures to add to his collection.

The Prince of Elboeuf watching workmen recovering sculptures

This late 18th-century painting shows the excavations at Pompeii. One of the theatres can be seen uncovered at the top of the ruins.

POMPEII UNEARTHED

Work on excavating Pompeii began in 1748. But the people digging were instructed to smash through the buildings in the hope of finding works of art and other treasures inside.

By the late 18th century, the area around Vesuvius had become a popular destination for rich tourists.

THE POMPEII EFFECT

The discoveries had a great influence on European interior design. Rooms were decorated in 'Pompeiian style', inspired by the wall paintings uncovered in the two cities.

Inside the Theatre Royal in London, where the design was influenced by Pompeiian style

GROWING INTEREST

Gradually, scholars became interested not only in the works of art found at the two sites, but what the discoveries revealed about the lives of the people there.

This detail of the mosaic shows the face of Alexander the Great.

In 1831, a huge mosaic was uncovered showing the Battle of Issus in 333 BC between Alexander the Great of Macedonia and King Darius of Persia. This was one of the most spectacular discoveries made in Pompeii.

RAISING THE DEAD

In 1860, an Italian scientist called Giuseppe Fiorelli was appointed head of excavations. He introduced new archaeological methods and made detailed records of the work.

Fiorelli devised a method of making plaster casts of the bodies. He realized that while the bodies had rotted away, their outlines had been preserved as cavities in the ash.

1. When the volcano erupted, the body was covered in ash and stones.

2. Then it rotted away, leaving its outline preserved.

3. Archaeologists drilled a hole and poured in liquid plaster.

4. The ash was chipped away to reveal a plaster cast of the body inside.

THE CITIES TODAY

Hundreds of thousands of tourists visit Pompeii and Herculaneum every year. The large number of visitors is putting a huge strain on the ruins, and the sites are suffering as a result. In the future, experts will have to find ways of allowing people access to our archaeological inheritance, without placing these amazing discoveries at risk.

INDEX

USBORNE QUICKLINKS

For links to websites where you can find out more about the discoveries at Pompeii and the eruption of Vesuvius, go to the Usborne Quicklinks website at www.usborne.com/quicklinks and type in the keyword "Pompeii". Please follow the internet safety guidelines at the Usborne Quicklinks website.

ACKNOWLEDGEMENTS

Every effort has been made to trace and acknowledge ownership of copyright. If any rights have been omitted, the publishers offer to rectify this in any future editions following notification. The publishers are grateful to the following individuals and organizations for their permission to reproduce material on the following pages: t=top, m=middle, b=bottom, r=right, l=left

Cover: t DeAgostini Picture Library/Scala, Florence; bl © Walter Rawlings/Robert Harding/Getty Images; br © Alberto Pizzoli/Sygma/Corbis, **p4-5 Pompeii AD79:** p4tr © The Art Archive/Alamy; p5tl © Mimmo Jodice/Corbis; p5tr DeAgostini Picture Library/Scala, Florence; p5bl © The Art Archive/Alamy; p5br © Peter Horree/Alamy, **p6-7 Public Buildings:** p6bl © The Art Archive/Alamy; p6br © Andalucian Plus Image Bank/Alamy; p7tl Museo Archeologico Nazionale, Naples, Italy/Alinari/The Bridgeman Art Library; p7m © Alberto Pizzoli/Sygma/Corbis; p7br Photo Scala, Florence/Fotografica Foglia - courtesy of the Ministero Beni e Att. Culturali, **p8-9 A Villa in Pompeii:** p8bl © Stock Connection Blue/Alamy; p8br © The Art Archive/Alamy; p9tl Photo Scala, Florence - courtesy of the Ministero Beni e Att. Culturali; p9m DeAgostini Picture Library/Scala, Florence; p9bl Photo Scala, Florence - courtesy of the Ministero Beni e Att. Culturali, **p10-11 Trades and Crafts:** p10tr DeAgostini Picture Library/Scala, Florence; p10bl Photo Scala, Florence/Fotografica Foglia - courtesy of the Ministero Beni e Att. Culturali; p10br Photo Scala, Florence/Fotografica Foglia - courtesy of the Ministero Beni e Att. Culturali; p11tl C.M. Dixon/Ancient Art & Architecture Collection Ltd; p11ml Photo Scala, Florence; p11m © The Art Gallery Collection/Alamy; p11mr Photo Scala, Florence/Fotografica Foglia - courtesy of the Ministero Beni e Att. Culturali; p11br © The Art Archive/Alamy, **p12-13 Farming and Food:** p12tl Photo Scala, Florence/Fotografica Foglia - courtesy of the Ministero Beni e Att. Culturali; p12mr © Museo della Civilta Romana, Rome, Italy/The Bridgeman Art Library; p12bl © The Gallery Collection/Corbis; p13tl DeAgostini Picture Library/Scala, Florence; p13mr Samuel Magal/Getty Images, **p14-15 Wining and Dining:** p14tr Photo Scala, Florence - courtesy of the Ministero Beni e Att. Culturali; p14bl © Adam Eastland Italy/Alamy; p15tl © Adam Eastland Art + Architecture/Alamy; p15mr Photo Scala, Florence; p15m akg-images/Erich Lessing; p15br © The Art Archive/Alamy, **p16-17 Gods of Pompeii:** p16mr © Nick Fielding/Alamy; p16bl Photo Scala, Florence/Fotografica Foglia - courtesy of the Ministero Beni e Att. Culturali; p16br © Peter Horree/Alamy; p17tl © The Art Archive/Alamy; p17m © The Art Archive/Alamy; p17br © Mimmo Jodice/Corbis, **p18-19 Looking Good:** p18m Photo Scala, Florence/Fotografica Foglia - courtesy of the Ministero Beni e Att. Culturali; p18bl Photo Scala, Florence/Fotografica Foglia - courtesy of the Ministero Beni e Att. Culturali; p18br Photo Scala, Florence/Fotografica Foglia - courtesy of the Ministero Beni e Att. Culturali; p19tl © De Agostini/Getty Images; p19mr © Peter Horree/Alamy; p19ml © The Art Archive/Alamy; p19bl © The Art Archive/Alamy; p19br © The Art Archive/Alamy, **p20-21 Growing Up:** p20tr © Trustees of The British Museum; p20m © Araldo de Luca/Corbis; p20mr © Trustees of The British Museum; p20bl © The Art Archive/Alamy; p21tr Photo Scala, Florence/Fotografica Foglia - courtesy of the Ministero Beni e Att. Culturali; p21ml © The Art Archive/Alamy, **p22-23 Health and Medicine:** p22ml DeAgostini Picture Library/Scala, Florence; p22b DeAgostini Picture Library/Scala, Florence; p22br © Peter Horree/Alamy; p23tr © The Art Archive/Alamy; p23ml © The Art Archive/Alamy; p23br © The Art Archive/Alamy, **p24-25 Entertainment:** p24mr © The Art Archive/Alamy; p24br © Peter Horree/Alamy; p25tl © Araldo de Luca/Corbis; p25tr DeAgostini Picture Library/Scala, Florence; p25ml © The Art Archive/Alamy; p25bl © The Art Gallery Collection/Alamy; p25br Leemage/Getty Images, **p26-27 Destruction:** p26bl © Jonathan Blair/Corbis; p26br © Mimmo Jodice/Corbis; © National Geographic Image Collection/Alamy; p27tl © Andrew Bargery/Alamy; p27ml © David Sutherland/Corbis; p27mr © Walter Rawlings/Robert Harding/Getty Images, **p28-29 Herculaneum:** p28m © Alex Ramsay/Alamy; p28bl DeAgostini Picture Library/Scala, Florence; p28bm Photo Scala, Florence/Fotografica Foglia - courtesy of the Ministero Beni e Att. Culturali; p28br © Erin Babnik/Alamy; p29tr © David Coleman/Alamy; p29ml DeAgostini Picture Library/Scala, Florence; p29bl © National Geographic Image Collection/Alamy, **p30-31 Discovery:** p30ml © National Trust Photographic Library/John Hammond/The Bridgeman Art Library; p30br © Historical Picture Archive/Corbis; p31tr DeAgostini Picture Library/Scala, Florence; p31b © Vanni Archive/Corbis

Edited by Jane Chisholm and Rachel Firth
Managing Designer: Stephen Moncrieff
With thanks to Ruth King
Digital manipulation by John Russell